Core Knowledge®

ISBN: 978-1-68380-292-1

Canada

Table of Contents

Reader

Core Knowledge History and Geography™

Chapter 1
Visiting Canada

A Letter from Sam Dear Mom and Dad, I'm having a great time here in Toronto, Ontario. Aunt Susie and Uncle Rick are taking good care of me. Cousin Joe is fun to play with, and Cousin Margaret is really smart and tells me lots of neat stuff.

The Big Question

What are some similarities and differences between Canada and the United States today?

I have to admit I was a little nervous when I came here last week. You said I'd have a great time visiting our Canadian relatives. You showed me on a map that Canada is the country just north of the United States. It was then that I saw that Toronto is *very* far away from our house in Liberal, Kansas. When the plane I was traveling on arrived at the airport in Toronto, I thought to myself, "I really am a long way from Kansas!"

I was afraid that when I got here, people would be wearing different clothes and speaking a language I don't understand. And what about the food? I worried that Canadians might eat food I don't like! It turns out the food is not that different. On my first day here,

Vocabulary

province, n. a political area or region in Canada similar to a state

Toronto is one of the largest cities in Canada. It is located in the **province of Ontario.**

I ate pancakes for breakfast and pizza for lunch. I had chocolate ice cream, too!

In many ways it's just like home here! People speak English in Toronto. The neighborhood even looks like our neighborhood back home. Best of all, they have some of my favorite TV shows, too!

Canada's Provinces and Territories

As you can see, Canada is a large country. It is made up of ten provinces and three territories. Can you find Toronto, Ontario, where Sam is visiting?

On my second day here, Aunt Susie took me to the grocery store. At the checkout counter the clerk said, "That'll be thirty dollars and eighty-two cents, please."

I thought, 'Wow! Even the money here is just like the money back home—dollars and cents.' I was starting to wonder whether I'd really left home at all.

Vocabulary

territory, n. an area of land governed in part by the Canadian parliament

But then I noticed some things *are* different. As we were leaving the grocery store, Aunt Susie said, "Sam, would you like to

The Canadian twenty-dollar bill

see some Canadian money?" She handed me some paper money. I saw right away that it wasn't like American money. On the front of a twenty-dollar bill was a picture of a woman I'd never seen before. "That's the British queen," Aunt Susie said.

I asked why the British queen was on Canadian money.

Aunt Susie said, "I know you study American history at school. You know that hundreds of years ago, the United States began as thirteen English **colonies**. However, the English settled in Canada, too. I am sure you know that in the 1700s, the Americans fought a revolution to free themselves. Of course, by the time the American Revolution happened, England had become Great Britain and you were fighting the British. The thirteen colonies became the United States of America. But Canada stayed as a British colony. Today we're an independent country, but we're still proud of our British **culture**. In fact, we say that the British monarch is Canada's "**head of state**."

"Does that mean she's in charge?" I asked.

> ## Vocabulary
>
> **colony,** n. an area, region, or country that is controlled and settled by people from another country
>
> **culture,** n. the language, religion, customs, traditions, and material possessions of a group of people
>
> **head of state,** n. a country's leader

"No, not at all," Aunt Susie said. "Like the United States, Canada is a **republic**. The people rule through their **elected representatives**. Our top official is called the **prime minister**. He has about the same power as your president. Look, here's a one-dollar coin. It has the queen's picture on it, too." I looked at the gold-colored coin she handed me. On one side was a picture of the queen. On the other side was a picture of a bird that looked sort of like a duck. "That bird is a loon," Aunt Susie said. "We call the one-dollar coin a loonie."

I laughed and said it sounded like a funny name for money. She laughed, too. "I guess you're right," she said. "But that picture shows something important about Canada. You know, Canada is a large country, even larger than the United States. But compared to the United States, it has far fewer people. Much of Canada is wilderness—wild country where no people live. The wilderness is full of animals, including the loon. Like a duck, it lives on lakes. Look, here's another Canadian animal. Do you know what it is?"

She handed me a five-cent coin. I saw a picture of a furry animal with a wide, flat tail, but I couldn't tell what it was. Aunt Susie said it was a beaver. "You know, beavers are amazing animals. They can gnaw down trees with their teeth. They were very important in Canadian history. In the days when Canada was a colony, thousands of people came from Europe because of them."

The Canadian wilderness is home to animals such as the loon and the beaver.
These animals are shown on one side of Canadian coins.

"Why? Did they want to see beavers chop down trees with their teeth?" I asked.

Aunt Susie laughed. She said, "No. It was because in Europe in those days, the most popular kind of hat was made from beaver fur. People could make a lot of money selling the fur, so they came here to trap the beavers."

It doesn't sound like a lot of fun being made into a hat.

When we got back to Aunt Susie's house, Cousin Margaret was watching TV. The people on the TV were speaking, but I couldn't understand what they were saying.

Margaret saw that I was puzzled. She said, "They're speaking French. In fact, on this TV channel, *all* the shows are in French."

Margaret told me that in Canada, there are two main languages. She explained that most of the people in Ontario speak English as their main language. In some other parts of Canada, the people speak French as their main language. But all Canadians study both English and French in school.

Margaret turned off the TV and asked, "What do you know about the people of Canada?"

"Not much," I said.

"Well, how about we fix that," she said. "Did you know that Canada is a **multicultural** country? The largest group of Canadians is made up of people whose ancestors were settlers from England. The second-largest group are the people whose ancestors were from France. But lots of other groups settled here, too. On the west coast of Canada, there are many people whose families came from countries in Asia, such as China. Many of them speak an Asian language as well as English or French.

"However, the people who have been here the longest are the **indigenous** peoples. They were here long, long before the English

Hockey is a very popular sport in Canada.

8

and the French came to Canada. For years most people called them Indians, but now many Canadian indigenous groups prefer to be called either First Nations or First Peoples.

The maple leaf, shown here on the Canadian flag, is Canada's national symbol.

The things Margaret told me are very interesting. "There is one other thing I have noticed since being here: Canadians seem to know *a lot* about ice and snow. Cousin Joe says that even here in southern Canada, it's freezing cold most of the winter. Joe likes the snow and ice because winter is hockey season. He's got his own hockey stick, skates, and pads, and there are pictures of hockey players all over his bedroom walls. Canadians seem to be as crazy about hockey as Americans are about baseball and football.

So, Mom and Dad, don't worry about me. I'm having fun and learning a lot about Canada. I'm still glad that the food's not too different, though. In fact, do you know what the national **symbol** of Canada is? It's the leaf from the maple tree—the tree whose sap is used to make syrup for pancakes. And you know how much I love maple syrup. Every time I see a Canadian flag with a maple leaf on it, I get a little hungry!

Love,

Sam

> **Vocabulary**
>
> **symbol,** n. a picture or object that is a sign for something; for example, the American flag is a symbol of the United States.

Chapter 2
The Story of Canada

Two Languages Sam discovered that French and English are the two main languages of Canada. This is because, as early as the 1500s, many people from France and England **settled** in Canada.

However, by the time the Europeans arrived, people had already lived in Canada for thousands of years. When the Europeans came, they met many different groups of people. The different groups had their own customs, traditions, languages, and religions.

In the far north of Canada, in the Canadian **Arctic**, lived the people called the **Inuit** (/in*yoo*it/). They still live there today. The Inuit have a rich culture. For most of the year, the Canadian Arctic is covered with ice and snow, but the Inuit have learned how to survive there with limited **resources**.

The Big Question

What kinds of things do Canada and the United States share in their histories?

Vocabulary

settle, v. to move to a new place and make it home

Arctic, n. the region of the Arctic Ocean, including the land in and around it

Inuit, n. a group of indigenous people from northern Canada, formerly known as Eskimo

resource, n. something that people can use

The Inuit are an indigenous people who have lived in northern Canada for thousands of years.

First Peoples

For hundreds of years, the Inuit hunted whales, walruses, seals, and polar bears. When the sea was frozen, they fished in it by cutting holes in the ice.

The Inuit traveled across the snow on sleds pulled by dogs. When they were far from home, they made shelters out of blocks of snow. These snow houses were called **igloos**. Today, life for the Inuit people has changed a lot.

The western coast of the country isn't as cold and snowy. Unlike the north, it is covered with trees. The people who lived there made their houses out of wood. They also used wood to make many other items. One important item was a **totem pole**. A totem pole is a tall post with carved designs of animals and people. Totem poles are part of the traditional religions.

Vocabulary

igloo, n. a dome-shaped, temporary shelter made from snow blocks

totem pole, n. a tall, wooden pole with carvings of people and animals used by the people of western Canada for religious purposes

Totem poles are part of the indigenous culture of western Canada.

In the center of Canada are wide open plains. The people in this area survived by hunting buffalo. The people of the plains were always moving, following the buffalo herds. So they invented a kind of house that they could pick up and take with them. This was a cone-shaped tent called a **tepee**.

The eastern coast of Canada was home to people who lived by hunting and farming. Unlike the people of the plains, the people of the eastern coast of Canada settled in one place. They lived in big homes called **longhouses**. These were the people the European explorers and settlers met when they sailed across the Atlantic in the late 1400s and early 1500s.

Europeans Come to Canada

Before the 1400s, the Vikings reached the coastal areas of northeastern Canada, and in particular northern Newfoundland. Then in the late 1400s, explorers trying to get to Asia bumped into the huge continents of North and South America. These European explorers hoped to find a way to Asia by sailing across the Atlantic Ocean. Asia had valuable things that Europeans wanted— gold, jewels, and spices. Instead of Asia, they found North and South America— and therefore Canada. First English and then French explorers came to Canada.

> **Vocabulary**
>
> **tepee,** n. a cone-shaped tent used by people who lived on the plains of central Canada
>
> **longhouse,** n. a large rectangular dwelling with doors located at each end and places for fires inside

At first the English and the French were disappointed not to find gold and jewels. But soon they found that Canada had other things to offer, such as fish and beaver fur. Fish and beaver fur don't sound as exciting as gold and jewels. Still, they *were* valuable. The Atlantic Ocean off the coast of Canada was full of fish that could be dried and sent back to Europe for people to eat. Rich Europeans were willing to pay a lot of money for hats made from beaver fur.

The English and the French settled in different places. The English settled mainly on the Atlantic Coast. The French settled the area along the St. Lawrence River. On the banks of the St. Lawrence, they built two cities, Montreal and Quebec (/kwuh*bek/). They called their part of this land New France.

The English and the French were interested in the rich fishing areas along Canada's Atlantic Coast.

War in Canada

Then, in the 1700s, war broke out between the British and the French. At first they fought only in Europe. Eventually, British and French armies were fighting in Canada, too. In 1759, the British attacked Quebec, the main city of New France—the name given to the French settled area at this time. The French soldiers had a strong position, on top of a tall cliff. But the British had a plan! They sailed up the river at night and climbed the cliffs. The fighting left many soldiers dead. In fact, both the British general and the French general were killed. The British won the battle and took control of all of New France.

Now all of Canada was ruled by the British, even though many French people still lived there. The British promised that the French people could keep their culture, including their language. And that is what they did!

Rebellion

As you know, people in the British colonies to the south of Canada rebelled in 1776. They declared that they were then a new country called the United States of America.

However, not all of the American colonists wanted to break away from Britain. Thousands of these colonists moved north to Canada. There, they could stay under British rule. These people became known as Tories or Loyalists. The Americans thought these people were traitors. The Canadians thought they were being true to their king.

Canada Expands West

In the 1800s, Canada spread westward, all the way to the Pacific Ocean. (The United States was spreading westward at the same time.) European Canadians settled areas where only indigenous peoples had lived before. They often treated these people badly, pushing them off their land. But one group of Canadians became known for treating the indigenous peoples with respect. This group was the Royal Canadian Mounted Police, or Mounties.

The Royal Canadian Mounted Police, or Mounties, were organized in the late 1800s.

In the late 1800s, western Canada was like the Wild West in the United States. It was a violent place, where people often broke the law because there was no one to stop them. The Mounties were set up to bring law and order to the area and to help protect the indigenous people. Wearing bright red uniforms, the Mounties rode on horses to track down criminals. They were so brave and so good at catching criminals that they became heroes to people all over the country.

Independence for Canada

Over time, Canada, like the United States, broke away from Britain. But it did so without a revolution. In the late 1800s and early 1900s, the British government gave Canadians more say in running their country. Today Canada is an independent country like the United States.

Chapter 3
Places in Canada

Many Kinds of Land Canada is on the North American continent, just north of the United States. Like the United States, Canada stretches all the way from the Atlantic Ocean to the Pacific Ocean. However, Canada is even bigger than the United States.

The Big Question

How might people take advantage of the resources found in the places where they live?

In fact, it's the world's second-largest country in land size. Only Russia is bigger. But this large country has a small population. Although the United States is smaller in size than Canada, it has many more people.

The main reason that Canada has so few people is its **climate**. Northern Canada is very, very cold in the winter. Because northern Canada is so cold, most Canadians live in the south, near the U.S. border.

Atlantic Provinces

Canada is divided into areas called provinces and territories. There are ten provinces, each with its own **capital**. On the Atlantic Coast are the provinces of New Brunswick, Nova Scotia,

Vocabulary

climate, n. the usual weather of a place, including its temperature and precipitation

capital, n. the home of a country's government and a main city in a country

18

The climate and landscape of Canada affect where and how people live.

Prince Edward Island, and Newfoundland and Labrador. These provinces were settled in the 1500s by the English and French. These settlers caught fish to send back to Europe. Today, many people there still make a living fishing.

A visitor to this area would see lots of fishing villages and small harbors full of boats. You also might see something very exciting—a whale. This area of the Atlantic Ocean is home to these huge mammals. Many people take boats out to sea, hoping to get a close-up look at a whale.

Canada's Provinces and Territories (Aerial View)

Canada has ten provinces and three territories.

Quebec and Ontario

West of the Atlantic Provinces is a large province called Quebec. Most people in this province speak French. Many street signs are also in French. The people of Quebec are very proud of their language and traditions. So if you meet someone in Quebec, say *"bonjour"* (/bon*zhoor/) instead of "hello"!

Quebec is home to two important cities, Montreal and Quebec City. Both are located on the St. Lawrence River. Quebec City is the capital of Quebec. It's a very beautiful place, full of old buildings from the 1700s and 1800s. Some of the buildings look like the ones you would see in European cities.

To the west of Quebec is the province of Ontario. More people live here than in any other province. Canada's capital city, Ottawa, is in Ontario. So is its largest city, Toronto. Toronto is full of tall, modern buildings.

Middle and Western Provinces

In the middle of Canada is the province of Manitoba. Manitoba has huge lakes and beautiful forests. Its capital city is Winnipeg. Manitoba was once a center for beaver trapping. But the most famous animal from Manitoba wasn't a beaver; it was a little black bear who became the pet of a Canadian soldier. The soldier took the bear to London, England, and gave it to the London Zoo.

One day, an English writer saw the bear in the zoo. He noticed that the bear's name was Winnie. (The Canadian soldier had named her

A Canadian bear inspired A.A. Milne to create the character Winnie-the-Pooh.

after his hometown, Winnipeg.) When the writer A.A. Milne wrote a story about an imaginary bear, he called his bear Winnie-the-Pooh.

West of Manitoba are the provinces of Saskatchewan (/sa*skach*uh*won/) and Alberta. Saskatchewan has wide, flat plains on which farmers grow wheat. In Alberta they grow wheat too, and they also raise cattle. As in the United States, people who help raise cattle are called cowboys. Now, the oil **industry** has become very important in this area.

On the western coast of Canada is the province of British Columbia. The Rocky Mountains run through the eastern part of the province. These are the same Rockies that run through the western United States. Much of the land is forest. Many people there cut down trees for **lumber**.

Northern Territories

The northwestern part of Canada is divided into three territories. These are the Yukon Territory, the Northwest Territories, and Nunavut (/nu*na*vut/). The Yukon Territory is named for the Yukon River, which flows through Canada and Alaska. In the late 1800s, gold was discovered there. People from all over the world hoped to get rich by finding gold. But most of them went home disappointed. Today the Yukon has a small population. Even fewer people live in the Northwest Territories and Nunavut.

These areas are covered with ice and snow for eight months of the year. The Hudson Bay, a large body of water south of Nunavut and named after English explorer Henry Hudson, is frozen part of the year. Many of the people who live in these territories are Inuit. In fact, Nunavut has been set aside as a special Inuit homeland. (Nunavut means "Our Land" in the Inuit language.) In many ways,

Some Inuit still hunt caribou, just as their ancestors did thousands of years ago.

the lives of the Inuit have changed. Today most Inuit houses are made of wood, not snow. And the Inuit now are more likely to

ride around on snowmobiles than dogsleds. But the Inuit still hunt the same animals their ancestors hunted. If you were invited to an Inuit dinner, you might be served walrus, seal, or **caribou!**

A Close Neighbor

It's important for Americans to know about Canada because this country is our next-door neighbor. It's always good to know your neighbors. But Canada and the United States aren't just neighbors—they're also close friends. If you visit Canada, you will get a warm welcome. Canadians will be eager to show you around and tell you more about their country. If you go in the winter, remember to dress very warmly. Bring your coat and gloves. And you'll need a hat to keep your head warm—but it doesn't have to be made from beaver fur!

Glossary

A

Arctic, n. the region of the Arctic Ocean, including the land in and around it (10)

C

capital, n. the home of a country's government and a main city in a country (18)

caribou, n. a species of deer native to North America (23)

climate, n. the usual weather of a place, including its temperature and precipitation (18)

colony, n. an area, region, or country that is controlled and settled by people from another country (5)

culture, n. the language, religion, customs, traditions, and material possessions of a group of people (5)

E

"elected representative", (phrase) a person who is chosen, by vote, by the people to speak or act for them (6)

H

head of state, n. a country's leader (5)

I

igloo, n. a dome-shaped, temporary shelter made from snow blocks (12)

indigenous, adj. native to a particular area or environment (8)

industry, n. a business that manufactures a product or provides a service (22)

Inuit, n. a group of indigenous people from northern Canada, formerly known as Eskimo (10)

L

longhouse, n. a large rectangular dwelling with doors located at each end and places for fires inside (13)

lumber, n. wood that has been cut and is used for building (22)

M

multicultural, adj. including many different cultures (8)

P

prime minister, n. the person at the head of government in some countries (6)

province, n. a political area or region in Canada similar to a state (2)

R

republic, n. a kind of government where people elect representatives to rule for them (6)

resource, n. something that people can use (10)

S

settle, v. to move to a new place and make it home (10)

symbol, n. a picture or object that is a sign for something; for example, the American flag is a symbol of the United States. (9)

T

tepee, n. a cone-shaped tent used by people who lived on the plains of central Canada (13)

territory, n. an area of land governed in part by the Canadian parliament (4)

totem pole, n. a tall, wooden pole with carvings of people and animals used by the people of western Canada for religious purposes (12)

Exploration of North America

Table of Contents

Reader
Core Knowledge History and Geography™

Chapter 1
Early Spanish Explorers

Unexpected Finds Have you ever gone looking for one thing and ended up finding something completely different? Maybe you went into the woods to gather flowers but instead found a really interesting rock.

The Big Question

What were European explorers searching for when they sailed west?

Well, that is the way Europeans came upon North and South America. European explorers were searching for a shortcut to the East Indies. Instead, they found the West Indies and two continents.

You already know a little about one of these European explorers. Christopher Columbus was an Italian who explored for the king and queen of Spain. In 1492, Columbus led three ships out of a Spanish harbor and began sailing west.

Columbus Goes West

Columbus was looking for a shortcut to the East Indies. The East Indies was a group of islands in Asia where valuable **spices** grew.

Vocabulary

spice, n. a plant used to add flavor to food

Italian explorer Christopher Columbus sailed for Spain.

Columbus was guided by three beliefs. He believed that the world was round. He believed it was smaller than most people thought. He also believed that he could get from Europe to Asia and the East Indies by simply sailing westward across the Atlantic Ocean.

If Columbus had been taking a test, he would only have been able to answer one of the three questions correctly. It turned out that the world was round. Columbus had been right about that. But the world was much larger than Christopher Columbus ever imagined.

Columbus was sure he had reached the East Indies.

As for Columbus's third belief, it turned out that a large body of land stopped people from sailing directly to Asia. This body of land became known as the continents of North and South America.

On October 12, 1492, after more than a month of sailing, Columbus and his men sighted an island. Columbus went ashore and planted a flag in the sand to claim the island for the king and queen of Spain. He believed he had sailed all the way around the world to the East Indies. That was why he called the native people he met Indians.

A New World

In fact, Columbus had not found a new route to Asia. He had arrived in a land that was new to Europeans. It was not the world of spices that he had hoped to find. But it was still a very interesting place. The area became known as the West Indies.

During the early 1500s, many Spanish explorers came to this "New World." These explorers established **colonies** and began building a Spanish **empire**.

> **Vocabulary**
>
> **colony,** n. an area, region, or country that is controlled and settled by people from another country
>
> **empire,** n. a group of countries or territories under the control of one government or one ruler

Columbus himself sailed to this new world four times. He set up a colony on Hispaniola, an island in the Caribbean Sea. Today that island is the location of two countries: Haiti and the Dominican Republic.

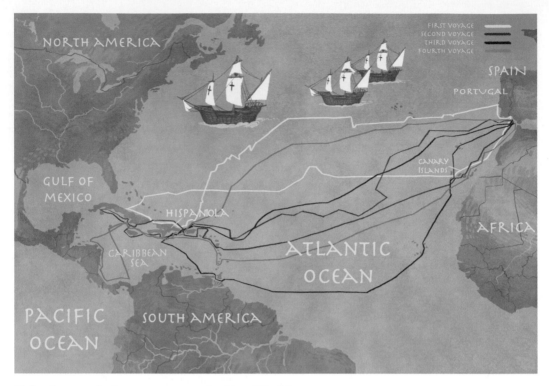

Columbus made four voyages to the New World.

Later, the Spanish set up colonies in other areas of the Caribbean. Spanish colonies were created on the islands of Cuba and Puerto Rico, along the northern coast of South America, and on the shores of the Gulf of Mexico. The Spaniards conquered the Inca people of Peru and the Aztec people of Mexico. They also began to explore lands that are part of the present-day United States.

Ponce de León

Juan Ponce de León (/hwan/pons*ay/day/lay*own/) was the first Spaniard to explore lands that later became part of the United States. Ponce de León, like Columbus, was looking for one thing. He ended up finding something else.

Ponce de León was born in Spain. Many historians think that he sailed to the Americas with Christopher Columbus on Columbus's second voyage. In any case, by 1502, Ponce de León was in the Americas.

He helped the Spaniards take control of Hispaniola from Native Americans. A few years later, he led an **expedition** that explored and settled the island of Puerto Rico.

In Hispaniola and Puerto Rico, Ponce de León traded in gold and enslaved people. He became very rich. He had everything a man could want. Or did he?

During his travels in the Americas, Ponce de León heard stories about a magical island called Bimini. According to the stories, Bimini had gold and pearls, and was the home of a life-giving fountain.

Ponce de León imagined finding the Fountain of Youth.

It was said that anyone who drank water from it would stay healthy and young forever. It was called the Fountain of Youth.

Season of Flowers

In the spring of 1513, Ponce de León sailed north from Puerto Rico. He was eager to find the Fountain of Youth. One morning he reached an unknown coast. Anchoring his ship, he waded through the shallow water up onto a beach.

As Columbus had done, he claimed the land for Spain. And, like Columbus, he gave the land a new name. The Spanish call the Easter season *Pascua Florida,* which means "season of flowers." Ponce de León arrived on this land with beautiful flowers on Easter Sunday. So he named the area Florida.

Ponce de León was struck by the beauty of the place he called Florida.

Exploring Florida

For Ponce de León, Florida was a new land. But for the Native Americans who lived there, it was an ancient home. Native Americans, whom the Spanish called Indians, had lived in Florida for many generations. They hunted small animals, fished, and gathered plants, nuts, and shellfish.

Native Americans lived in villages near fresh water, firewood, and stones for making tools. They traded to get things they could not make or find for themselves. They developed many traditions and ceremonies. Their way of life had grown over thousands of years.

As Ponce de León explored the coast of Florida, he met Native Americans. Many of them were prepared to fight to keep their homes and way of life. Eventually Ponce de León returned to Puerto Rico, where he spent the next seven years.

In 1521, Ponce de León decided to return to Florida to finish what he had set out to do. He wanted to set up a Spanish colony there. But the Native Americans had the same response as before. They attacked Ponce de León and his crew. The Spaniards were unable to build a **settlement**. Instead, they fled to Cuba. Ponce de León was wounded in the fighting. He died in Cuba, without ever finding the Fountain of Youth.

> **Vocabulary**
>
> **settlement,** n. a small village

Chapter 2
De Soto's Long March

A Restless Man Another Spanish explorer who came upon interesting places in North America was Hernando de Soto. Like Ponce de León, de Soto was looking for riches. Instead, he came upon the most important river in North America.

The Big Question

What regions in North America did de Soto explore, and what was he looking for?

De Soto was born in Spain. He came to the Americas when he was only fourteen or fifteen years old. He became a soldier and explorer.

In the early 1530s, de Soto was part of a Spanish expedition that conquered the Inca empire in Peru, South America. De Soto was second in command to the expedition's leader, Francisco Pizarro (/fran*sees*koh/ pee*sar*roh/). Both Pizarro and de Soto became very rich. They **exploited** the people and the riches of Peru.

Vocabulary

exploit, v. to take unfair advantage of a person or group

De Soto took his riches from South America back to Spain. For several years, he lived quietly, enjoying his great wealth. Then in 1538, he set out again on another expedition to find more riches. His desire for more treasure was so great, he even helped pay for his own expedition.

De Soto and Pizarro took riches from the people of Peru and shipped them back to Spain.

The Spaniards Attack

De Soto sailed first to the West Indies. Then he headed for Florida. He landed on the west coast of Florida, not far from Tampa Bay. Once on land, de Soto and his men began marching north.

De Soto knew that Native Americans in Florida had fought against Ponce de León. So, he arrived in Florida with about six hundred men with European weapons. They were ready to use those weapons against the Native Americans.

The Native Americans who saw de Soto's men must have been surprised. The Spaniards traveled with animals the Native Americans had never seen before, including horses and pigs. The Spaniards also had metal tools and nails. They had guns and **armor**. These things were unknown to the Native Americans.

> **Vocabulary**
>
> **armor,** n. metal outer covering worn to protect the body in battle

Native Americans had not seen horses or armor before.

When the Spaniards attacked, the Native Americans fought bravely. But they could not hope to win against the soldiers' weapons. De Soto continued to march north. He and his men burned Native American villages, and they forced Native American prisoners into slavery.

It is easy to understand why the Native Americans of Florida were afraid of de Soto and his men. They wanted the Spaniards to leave them in peace. They told de Soto that the gold and silver he was looking for could be found farther north and perhaps farther west. Native Americans told de Soto to just march about ten days in this or that direction. Then he would find what he was looking for. De Soto decided to follow their advice.

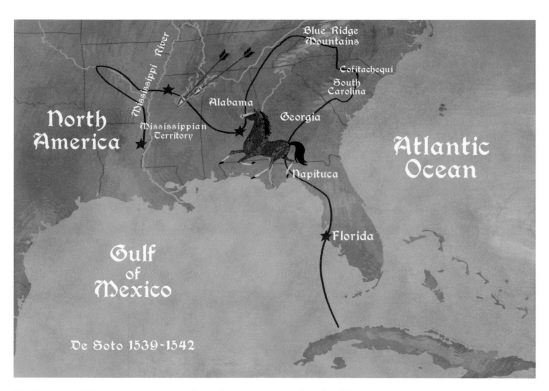

De Soto and his men went north and west in search of gold.

Sadly, although the Spanish moved on, they left **diseases** behind. Without knowing it, the Spaniards had brought diseases from Europe. Because the Native Americans had never faced these sicknesses before, their bodies could not fight them. Large numbers of Native Americans got sick and died. In the years after de Soto's journey in North America, European diseases killed thousands of Native Americans. One deadly disease was **smallpox**. Diseases, as it turned out, were more harmful to Native Americans than weapons.

As for de Soto, he soon found himself exploring much more territory than he had planned. His travels took him through areas in present-day Florida, Georgia, South Carolina, Alabama, Mississippi, and Arkansas.

The Mighty Mississippi

In May 1541, de Soto and his men became the first Europeans to see the river that Native Americans called Mississippi. This probably happened just south of present-day Memphis, Tennessee.

This was an exciting find. The Mississippi was (and still is) the most important river in North America. It flows from northern Minnesota all the way south to the Gulf of Mexico. Almost all of the rivers between the Appalachian Mountains and the Rocky Mountains flow into the Mississippi.

The Mississippi and the rivers that flow into it make up a network of rivers that was important to the Native Americans in de Soto's time.

Later, this network was very important to the **pioneers** and farmers who settled the American West. It remains very important to us today.

But de Soto did not understand the importance of his find. He had set out looking for gold, not rivers.

In 1542, de Soto caught a fever, grew ill, and died. His men wrapped up his body and placed it in the Mississippi River. Eventually some of de Soto's men floated down the river on rafts and made their way to Mexico.

Like so many Spanish expeditions in America, de Soto's expedition failed to find the gold he was looking for. But the expedition did lead to surprising finds. These discoveries paved the way for the further exploration of North America.

De Soto died in the land he had come to explore.

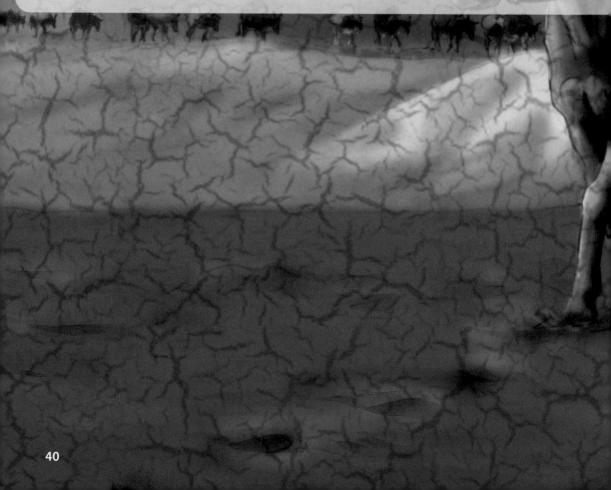

Chapter 3
The Search for El Dorado

A Golden City If you could have traveled with Spanish explorers in the 1500s, you might have heard stories about El Dorado. It was supposed to be a famous city of gold.

The Big Question

Why did Coronado and others explore what is now the American Southwest?

Coronado and other Spaniards traveled across the American Southwest.

Here are some stories you might have heard about El Dorado: El Dorado is a place of great mystery and magic. It is only found after a very long journey. To get there, you must travel for many months. You must cross rushing rivers. You must climb steep mountains. You must cross deep valleys and deserts.

You will see the kingdom for miles before you reach its borders. This is because it glows like a second sunrise in the light of day. You will see its silver towers first. Emeralds, rubies, and pearls shine like rainbows on every rooftop.

The chief of this wonderful kingdom is magnificent. He is covered in gold dust and wears a jeweled crown. Emeralds fall from his fingertips wherever he goes.

No one who lives in this kingdom is ever thirsty or hungry or sick. No one who lives there has any worries at all. The streets are always filled with dancing and singing. In the fountains in every square, precious stones gently drop into pools of liquid silver.

The Legend of El Dorado

The legend of El Dorado dates back to the arrival of the first Spanish explorers in the Americas. It was passed around among explorers for a long time. When little is known about a land, it is easy to believe all kinds of stories.

Many explorers called the city of gold, El Dorado. But others said its real name was perhaps Manoa (/mah*noh*ah/) or Quivira (/kee*vee*rah/) or Cibola (/cee*boh*lah/). Some people said

Explorers searched high and low for El Dorado.

there was only one city of gold. Other people insisted there were seven golden cities located near each other. They were called the Seven Cities of Cibola.

But the greatest mystery of all was the location of these cities. Indeed, the cities of gold seemed to move. As soon as one area had been explored, Europeans would decide that the cities must be somewhere else.

Explorers from all over Europe wanted to believe the legend. Each explorer wanted to be the one to claim this golden land for himself. They searched from the Amazon **rainforest** in South America to the **plains** of Kansas. They searched across the American Southwest. They followed the Rio Grande and climbed the peaks of the Rocky Mountains. The magnificent landscapes may have inspired them to continue their search. But for all of them, the search ended in disappointment.

> ## Vocabulary
>
> **rainforest,** n. a thick forest that gets a lot of rain and has very tall trees; the tops of the trees create an unbroken layer, or canopy, across the top
>
> **plain,** n. a large area of flat land that has few or no trees

Coronado

One man who heard stories about the cities of gold was Francisco Vásquez de Coronado (/fran*sees*koh/vas*kaysz/day/koh*roh*nah*doh/). Coronado was a Spanish official in Mexico. He had heard rumors about the Seven Cities of Cibola. He wanted to take them for Spain and for himself.

Coronado found Zuni villages instead of cities of gold.

In 1540, Coronado led an expedition north from Mexico into the American West. He took along three hundred soldiers, more than one thousand Native Americans, and huge herds of **livestock**. Coronado had what he thought was good information about where the Seven Cities of Cibola were located. But his search for gold and treasure ended in the main square of a small Zuni (/zoon*ee/) village.

When Coronado arrived, he urged the Zuni people to accept the Christian religion and pledge their loyalty to the king and queen of Spain. The Zuni people resisted. Coronado's men then overpowered them and drove them out of their own village.

Cibola turned out to be a big disappointment for the Spaniards. There were no golden towers, no walls plastered with silver, and no rubies and emeralds shining on rooftops. There were just some simple mud houses. The villages nearby were just the same. The Seven Cities of Cibola turned out to be seven little villages!

Coronado was disappointed, but he did not give up. He sent **scouting parties** out in various directions. One day in 1540, one of these parties came upon a gigantic, twisting **canyon**. The walls of the canyon rose up thousands of feet above the river, shining red, orange, and gold in the sun. Coronado's men were the first Europeans to see the Grand Canyon.

These men probably admired the Grand Canyon for a few minutes. But it was not long before they started thinking about the cities of gold again. They soon moved on.

Coronado and his men spent the winter on the river called the Rio Grande, which in Spanish means "big river." It is not far from where Santa Fe, New Mexico, is today. Then they continued their explorations.

Although Cibola had disappointed him, Coronado had heard rumors of another golden city called Quivira. He marched northeast to find this city. But when he got to the place where Native Americans had said Quivira was, he found only a small village of Wichita people in what is now Kansas.

This time, Coronado did give up on finding the cities of gold. In 1542, he returned to Mexico. Although he and his men had not found what they were looking for, they had gained great knowledge of this new land.

Chapter 4
Spanish North America

Florida In the 1500s and early 1600s, Spanish conquerors built a huge empire in the Americas. This empire included islands in the Caribbean Sea and large areas in Mexico, Central America, and South America.

The Big Question

Why did the Spanish decide to build settlements in North America, north of Mexico?

The Spanish needed to protect their treasure ships, so they decided to build settlements in Florida.

These Spanish conquerors were called **conquistadors** (/kon*kees*tuh*dorz/). At first they were not very interested in conquering North America. They had not found treasure there.

But their ambitions began to change. Spanish merchant ships often sailed from South America along the coast of Florida to Spain. These ships carried treasures from the settlements in South America back to Spain. English, Dutch, and French pirate ships began trying to capture the Spanish treasure ships. The Spaniards wanted to protect their ships. They decided the best way to do that was to set up forts and settlements along the coast of Florida in North America.

In 1565, a Spaniard named Pedro Menéndez de Avilés (/pay*droh/ may*nayn*des/day/ah*vee*lace/) landed 1,500 colonists on the northeastern coast of Florida. He landed not far from where Ponce de León had come ashore more than fifty years before. Menéndez achieved the goal that Ponce de León had not. He set up a successful Spanish colony in Florida. The colony was called St. Augustine. It still exists. It is the oldest continuing European settlement in the United States.

The Spaniards built similar settlements elsewhere in Florida. The **Roman Catholic Church** sent **priests** to build religious

The missions were a big part of Spain's plan to colonize parts of North America.

outposts called **missions**. Native Americans were brought in to do the work. Catholic priests taught the workers about Christianity. This kind of settlement helped Spain gain control of a wide area in Florida.

The Southwest and California

Spain also expanded its empire by moving north from Mexico into the American Southwest. Those areas are now Texas, Arizona, New Mexico, and Nevada. To do this, the Spaniards built a network of forts and missions. The forts were known as **presidios** (/prih*see*dee*ohz/). The forts helped the Spanish control Native Americans who rebelled against them.

Native Americans who joined the missions received food and a safe place to live. In return, they had to work and worship at the mission. They had to learn to live like the Spaniards. This meant they had to give up most of their old ways of life, including their religious beliefs.

Mission Life

Mission life centered on the church. The local priest was at the center of the community. The mission bell rang to tell people what to do during the day. The bell told them when to wake up, when to go to church, and when to pray. It even told them when it was time to work, to eat, to learn, or to sleep.

Most missions had a ranch for raising livestock, such as cattle, sheep, and goats. Native American men worked on these ranches, taking care of the animals. These men were called vaqueros (/vah*kehr*ohz/). They were the first cowboys.

Crops were raised on land near the mission. Native Americans worked the fields. The crops included corn, beans, chilies, squash, melons, and cotton. There were orchards and vineyards where apples, peaches, and grapes were grown.

Native Americans were also taught skills that helped keep the mission going. Carpenters, **blacksmiths**, and weavers were trained to meet the needs of the community. Women and girls made pottery and wove baskets. They also prepared the food for the big noontime meal.

The Spanish settlers set up many missions in the Southwest. One of the best known is San Antonio de Valero. It was founded in 1718. Today it is known as the Alamo. The Alamo played an important role in the later history of Texas.

In the 1700s, a Spanish priest named Father Junípero Serra (/hoo*nee*pay*roh/sehr*rah/) set up several missions in California.

Catholic priests taught Native Americans about the Christian religion. Some Spanish missions eventually became important cities.

Serra's dream was to establish a chain of missions that stretched all the way from Mexico to Alaska. Serra did not accomplish this goal. But many of the missions he founded became important cities. San Diego and San Francisco are just two examples.

The Pueblo Revolt

In some places relations between the Spanish settlers and Native Americans were friendly. In many other places, though, relations were not good. The Spaniards often used their weapons to conquer and enslave Native Americans. This caused great sorrow and anger for Native Americans. They suffered the loss of their freedom and the destruction of their traditional culture.

During the 1670s, the Spanish governor of New Mexico tried to force the Pueblo people to give up their religion and become Christians. Those who refused were either punished or killed.

One of the Pueblos who was punished was an important man named Popé (/pop*peh/). Popé responded by fighting back against the Spaniards. He said that the spirits of the Pueblo ancestors told him to drive away the Spanish settlers and their religion.

In 1680, Popé led a rebellion that included more than two dozen Pueblo communities. The groups involved in this rebellion lived in widely scattered villages and in some cases spoke different languages. But, they were united in their wish to drive out the Spaniards. They managed to push the Spaniards south to El Paso, Texas, and reclaim their territory.

The Pueblo Revolt led by Popé had succeeded. The Pueblos preserved their independence for twelve years after the revolt. But in 1692, the Spaniards took over New Mexico again. In the Southwest, and elsewhere in the Americas, European expansion was proving hard to stop.

Native Americans struggled to stop Europeans from taking their land.

Chapter 5
Exploring for England

Meet John Cabot John Cabot was born in Genoa. He was given the name Giovanni Caboto (/joh*vah*nee/kah*boh*toh/). Genoa is the Italian city where Christopher Columbus was born. As a young man, Cabot was a **merchant**. He traded goods in many ports. In 1490, Caboto moved his family to Spain. Perhaps he was hoping to go exploring.

The Big Question

What were John Cabot and Henry Hudson looking for?

At that time the Italians were not interested in sending explorers across the Atlantic. It was the Spaniards and the Portuguese who were interested in exploration. In 1492, the Spanish king and queen sent Columbus on his first voyage across the Atlantic Ocean. Meanwhile, the Portuguese were busy setting up **trading centers** on the route they controlled. That Portuguese route ran around the tip of Africa and across the Indian Ocean to India.

Vocabulary

merchant, n. a person who buys and sells goods to earn money

trading center, n. a place where people buy and sell goods

King Ferdinand and Queen Isabella were very interested in exploration because new discoveries might lead to more land and riches.

A New Found Land

Giovanni Caboto could not convince Spain or Portugal to send him exploring. So he moved to England. He settled in the port city of Bristol and changed his name to John Cabot. Finally, he persuaded King Henry VII of England to pay for him to sail out into the Atlantic.

Cabot set sail in May 1497, under an English flag. He chose a route that headed farther north than the route Columbus had taken only five years earlier. Five weeks after he left England, Cabot sighted land. Like Columbus, he believed that he had found an island near China. He named it New Found Land. Today it has the same name, but we write: Newfoundland (/new*fund*lund/). This land is located along the eastern coast of Canada.

Cabot returned to England with no spices or treasures to show King Henry. But he described the land that he had explored. In particular he described rich fishing waters. Cabot reported that there were so many fish that all you had to do to catch some was drop a basket in the water and pull it back up!

Cabot told King Henry about the great quantity of fish in the waters of Newfoundland.

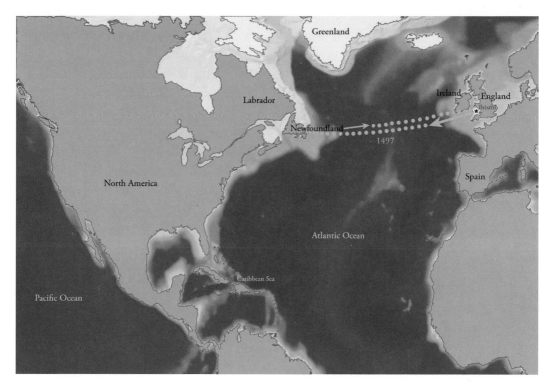

This map shows where historians believe Cabot sailed on his first voyage.

King Henry agreed to a second voyage for Cabot. But he would pay for only one ship. Merchants from Bristol paid for three more ships. They hoped that Cabot would find a new trade route to the Spice Islands.

Cabot's small **fleet** sailed in May 1498. This time he was determined to reach the Spice Islands of Asia. But he was never seen or heard from again. Perhaps he and his crew drowned in a storm. Or perhaps he and his crew were shipwrecked on some lonely coast where no one could rescue them.

Vocabulary

fleet, n. a group of ships sailing together with the same purpose and under the direction of the same leader

The Northwest Passage

When European explorers found the North American continent, they soon began to look for a way around it, or through it, so they could get to Asia. Christopher Columbus was looking for this shortcut, and so was John Cabot.

For hundreds of years, explorers looked for what they called the **Northwest Passage**. They believed that there had to be a sea route that would take them on to Asia. They could hardly wait to reach the Spice Islands and load their ships with valuable spices.

> **Vocabulary**
>
> **Northwest Passage,** n. a sea route connecting the Atlantic Ocean and Pacific Ocean

So they explored every river mouth that they found in North America. They sailed inland as far as they could. Sooner or later the rivers would become too narrow or too shallow. Often the water would freeze into ice and the explorers would have to turn back. But no matter how often they failed, they did not give up the search.

Even though these expeditions failed to find the Northwest Passage, they were valuable. Important knowledge about the land was gained on every journey.

Mapmakers used the new knowledge to make better, more accurate maps during the 1500s. European explorers began to understand the shape and size of North America. They realized that North America was so big that it should be called a continent.

Henry Hudson

More than one hundred years after John Cabot was lost at sea, an English explorer named Henry Hudson sailed through some of the same waters. He too, was trying to find a shortcut to Asia. Sometimes Hudson sailed for the English, and other times he sailed for the Dutch.

In 1609, Hudson got a job with the Dutch East India Company. The Dutch East India Company made a lot of money from the spice trade. They sent ships all the way around Africa to East Asia. But they wanted to find a quicker route to Asia. Hudson had ideas about finding a passage to the East.

While looking for the Northwest Passage in the far North, Henry Hudson and his crew had to deal with cold weather and icebergs.

Hudson's idea was to sail over the top of the world and along the northern coast of Russia. With a small crew, Hudson set sail on board a ship called the *Half Moon*.

He sailed the ship up the coast of Norway. As the *Half Moon* traveled farther north, the weather got worse and worse. It was very cold. The crew was not happy. To keep the crew from turning against him, Hudson changed the ship's course and headed toward North America.

A Great River

The *Half Moon* made it to North America and sailed down the Atlantic Coast, looking for a waterway that would lead to the Northwest Passage. This route took Hudson to the mouth of a great river. Could this be the way? Hudson explored the wide, deep channel. He claimed the land on its banks for Holland.

Today we call that waterway the Hudson River. It flows out of New York State and passes New York City, one of the world's greatest ports. But there were no cities along the river when Hudson sailed it.

The river did not lead to the Pacific Ocean, as Hudson had hoped it would. When the water became too shallow for the *Half Moon*, the disappointed Hudson turned the ship around and returned to Holland.

The Final Voyage

In the spring of 1610, Henry Hudson began another voyage on behalf of England. He sailed northwest in a new ship, the *Discovery*.

The weather was freezing cold. It got colder the farther north he went. The water became icy and dangerous. Hudson took *Discovery* past what is now Iceland and Greenland. After four months of travel, Hudson sailed into a great sea, which he thought was the Pacific Ocean. Excited by his find, Hudson kept going.

After three more months of westward travel, the weather grew even colder. Ice soon surrounded the ship. Food ran low, and the crew turned against Henry Hudson. In a **mutiny**, they forced him, his young son, and a few others into a small boat and then sailed home. They left Hudson in the bay that bears his name. He and his son were lost forever.

Henry Hudson's second trip to North America ended with a mutiny by his crew.

Chapter 6
Champlain and New France

The French Get Involved One of the greatest French explorers was Samuel de Champlain (/shame*plane/). Champlain made many voyages to North America in the early 1600s. Like Cabot and Hudson, he searched for the Northwest Passage.

The Big Question

What were some of the things that Champlain noticed about the St. Lawrence River Valley that made it a good place to settle?

Vocabulary

custom, n. a traditional way of acting or doing something

Champlain also made maps. He collected information about the things he saw. He observed Native Americans and reported on their **customs**.

On one trip, Champlain sailed south along the coast of what is now Maine. He eventually reached Cape Cod, in what is now Massachusetts. On a later trip, he sailed up the St. Lawrence River into what is now Canada.

Samuel de Champlain explored North America during the early 1600s.

A French Colony

Champlain liked the St. Lawrence River Valley right away because of the area's **natural resources**. Trees provided timber for building and fruit and nuts for food. There was grassland for raising livestock. There were berries, herbs, and roots for cooking. There were fish in the rivers and streams. And there were many different animals to hunt and trap in the forests and meadows. Champlain decided that this was the perfect spot to build the first permanent, or long-lasting, French colony in North America. And that is what he did. In 1608, he and thirty other Frenchmen established a **trading post** along the St. Lawrence River. Champlain named his outpost Quebec (/kwuh*bek/).

> **Vocabulary**
>
> **natural resource,** n. something from nature that is useful to humans
>
> **trading post,** n. a small settlement or store that is set up to sell or trade goods

The trading post of Quebec was established along the St. Lawrence River by Champlain in 1608.

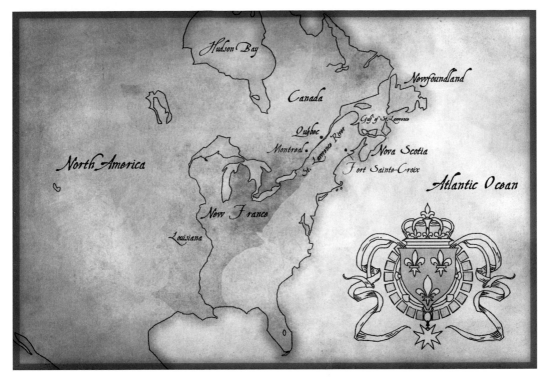

The settlement started by Champlain became the colony of New France.

Only nine of the original settlers survived the first winter. Still, Quebec eventually began to grow. Champlain and his men traded with Native Americans, offering knives and tools in exchange for beaver furs. The furs were shipped back to Europe, where beaver hats were very popular.

Eventually, the French set up more towns along the St. Lawrence River. Quebec became the center of the French colony known as New France.

The Great Lakes

The St. Lawrence River led Champlain and other French explorers deep into the North American continent. There they found five gigantic lakes. Today, we call these lakes the Great Lakes. They are so large that sailing on them feels like sailing on the ocean!

Champlain himself explored Lake Ontario and Lake Huron during the 1610s. Later in the 1600s, other French explorers came upon Lake Michigan, Lake Erie, and Lake Superior.

In 1678, a French priest who was living in the area between Lake Ontario and Lake Erie came upon Niagara Falls. It is one of the largest and most powerful waterfalls in the world. More than three hundred thousand tons of water pour over the edge of these amazing falls each minute!

Accidental Finds

One of the most remarkable things about the exploration of North America is how much was accomplished by accident. The French priest who came upon Niagara Falls was not looking for a waterfall. Columbus was not looking for the Caribbean. De Soto did not hope to find the Mississippi River. Coronado was looking for glittering cities, not glittering canyons. Cabot stumbled upon Newfoundland, but that was not the land he had hoped to find. Hudson was disappointed that neither the river nor the bay named for him led to Asia. Champlain hoped that the St. Lawrence River would lead him to Asia. It led him into the Great Lakes instead.

There is something inspiring about these stories. It shows that, when you explore, surprising things can happen. And this is true, no matter what you are exploring.

You might be sailing to other countries or just exploring your neighborhood. You might be exploring nature in a forest or park. Or you might be exploring other cultures by reading books or surfing the Web. No matter what you choose to explore, there is always a chance that you will find something remarkable and new. So keep on exploring!

Glossary

A

armor, n. metal outer covering worn to protect the body in battle (36)

B

blacksmith, n. a type of craftsperson who makes iron tools by hand (53)

C

canyon, n. a deep valley between mountains, cut through the rock by river water (46)

colony, n. an area, region, or country that is controlled and settled by people from another country (29)

conquistador, n. the Spanish word for conqueror (50)

custom, n. a traditional way of acting or doing something (64)

D

disease, n. sickness (38)

E

empire, n. a group of countries or territories under the control of one government or one ruler (29)

expedition, n. a special journey taken by a group that has a clear purpose or goal (31)

exploit, v. to take unfair advantage of a person or group (34)

F

fleet, n. a group of ships sailing together with the same purpose and under the direction of the same leader (59)

L

livestock, n. the animals kept on a farm (45)

M

merchant, n. a person who buys and sells goods to earn money (56)

mission, n. a settlement built for the purpose of converting Native Americans to Christianity (51)

mutiny, n. a rebellion of a ship's crew against the captain (63)

N

natural resource, n. something from nature that is useful to humans (66)

Northwest Passage, n. a sea route connecting the Atlantic Ocean and Pacific Ocean (60)

P

pioneer, n. one of the first people to settle in a region (39)

plain, n. a large area of flat land that has few or no trees (44)

presidio, n. a fort (52)

priest, n. a person who has the training or authority to carry out certain religious ceremonies or rituals (50)

R

rainforest, n. a thick forest that gets a lot of rain and has very tall trees; the tops of the trees create an unbroken layer, or canopy, across the top (44)

Roman Catholic Church, n. the branch of Christianity led by the pope, whose headquarters are in Rome, Italy (50)

S

"scouting party," (phrase) a few members of a group who are sent out ahead of the rest of the group to get information about an area (46)

settlement, n. a small village (33)

smallpox, n. a serious disease that spreads from person to person and causes a fever and rash (38)

spice, n. a plant used to add flavor to food (26)

T

trading center, n. a place where people buy and sell goods (56)

trading post, n. a small settlement or store that is set up to sell or trade goods (66)

Core Knowledge®

CKHG™
Core Knowledge HISTORY AND GEOGRAPHY™

Series Editor-In-Chief
E.D. Hirsch, Jr.

Editorial Directors
Linda Bevilacqua and Rosie McCormick

Canada

Subject Matter Expert

Charles F. Gritzner, PhD, Distinguished Professor Emeritus of Geography, South Dakota State Universityw

Illustration and Photo Credits

Cover Image, Totem Pole: Neale Clark/robertharding/SuperStock; Cover Image, Inuit Girl: Wolfgang Kaehler/Superstock

1 dollar coin, 1993, Reverse, Great northern loon (Gavia immer), Canada, 20th century / De Agostini Picture Library / A. Dagli Orti / Bridgeman Images: 7

Alan Alexander Milne (1882-1956) english novelist Alan Alexander Milne who wrote the story of Winnie the Pooh (1926) here with his son Christopher Robin Milne , picture by Howard Coster, 1926 / Photo © PVDE / Bridgeman Images: 21

CCOphotostock_KMN/Prisma/SuperStock: 18–19

Dave Reede/All Canada Photos/SuperStock: 8

Don Johnston/age fotostock/SuperStock: 23

imageBROKER/SuperStock: 5

Ivan Vdovin/age fotostock/SuperStock: 7

Marti Major: 14

Neale Clark/robertharding/SuperStock: 12

Radius/SuperStock: 1, 9

robertharding/SuperStock: i, iii, 3

Ton Koene/age fotostock/SuperStock: 16

Universal Images Group/SuperStock: 20

WALT DISNEY PICTURES/Album/SuperStock: 21

Wolfgang Kaehler/Superstock: Cover, 10–11

Exploration of North America

Subject Matter Experts

Matthew M. Davis, PhD, University of Virginia

Tony Williams, Senior Teaching Fellow, Bill of Rights Institute

Illustration and Photo Credits